On the Art of Poetry

Aristotle
Translated by Ingram Bywater

On the Art of Poetry

Copyright © 2020 by Bibliotech Press
All rights reserved

The present edition is a reproduction of previous publication of this classic work. Minor typographical errors may have been corrected without note, however, for an authentic reading experience the spelling, punctuation, and capitalization have been retained from the original text.

ISBN: 978-1-61895-866-2

Preface

In the tenth book of the Republic, when Plato has completed his final burning denunciation of Poetry, the false Siren, the imitator of things which themselves are shadows, the ally of all that is low and weak in the soul against that which is high and strong, who makes us feed the things we ought to starve and serve the things we ought to rule, he ends with a touch of compunction: 'We will give her champions, not poets themselves but poet-lovers, an opportunity to make her defense in plain prose and show that she is not only sweet—as we well know—but also helpful to society and the life of man, and we will listen in a kindly spirit. For we shall be gainers, I take it, if this can be proved.' Aristotle certainly knew the passage, and it looks as if his treatise on poetry was an answer to Plato's challenge.

Few of the great works of ancient Greek literature are easy reading. They nearly all need study and comment, and at times help from a good teacher, before they yield up their secret. And the Poetics cannot be accounted an exception. For one thing the treatise is fragmentary. It originally consisted of two books, one dealing with Tragedy and Epic, the other with Comedy and other subjects. We possess only the first. For another, even the book we have seems to be unrevised and unfinished. The style, though luminous, vivid, and in its broader division systematic, is not that of a book intended for publication. Like most of Aristotle's extant writing, it suggests the MS. of an experienced lecturer, full of jottings and adscripts, with occasional phrases written carefully out, but never revised as a whole for the general reader. Even to accomplished scholars the meaning is often obscure, as may be seen by a comparison of the three editions recently published in England, all the work of savants of the first eminence, [1] or, still more strikingly, by a study of the long series of misunderstandings and overstatements and corrections which form the history of the Poetics since the Renaissance.

But it is of another cause of misunderstanding that I wish principally to speak in this preface. The great edition from which the present translation is taken was the fruit of prolonged study by one of the greatest Aristotelians of the nineteenth century, and is itself a classic among works of scholarship. In the hands of a student who knows even a little Greek, the translation, backed by the

---

[1] Prof. Butcher, 1895 and 1898; Prof. Bywater, 1909; and Prof. Margoliouth, 1911.

commentary, may lead deep into the mind of Aristotle. But when the translation is used, as it doubtless will be, by readers who are quite without the clue provided by a knowledge of the general habits of the Greek language, there must arise a number of new difficulties or misconceptions.

To understand a great foreign book by means of a translation is possible enough where the two languages concerned operate with a common stock of ideas, and belong to the same period of civilization. But between ancient Greece and modern England there yawn immense gulfs of human history; the establishment and the partial failure of a common European religion, the barbarian invasions, the feudal system, the regrouping of modern Europe, the age of mechanical invention, and the industrial revolution. In an average page of French or German philosophy nearly all the nouns can be translated directly into exact equivalents in English; but in Greek that is not so. Scarcely one in ten of the nouns on the first few pages of the Poetics has an exact English equivalent. Every proposition has to be reduced to its lowest terms of thought and then re-built. This is a difficulty which no translation can quite deal with; it must be left to a teacher who knows Greek. And there is a kindred difficulty which flows from it. Where words can be translated into equivalent words, the style of an original can be closely followed; but no translation which aims at being written in normal English can reproduce the style of Aristotle. I have sometimes played with the idea that a ruthlessly literal translation, helped out by bold punctuation, might be the best. For instance, premising that the words poesis, poetes mean originally 'making' and 'maker', one might translate the first paragraph of the Poetics thus:—

MAKING: kinds of making: function of each, and how the Myths ought to be put together if the Making is to go right.

Number of parts: nature of parts: rest of same inquiry.

Begin in order of nature from first principles.

Epos-making, tragedy-making (also comedy), dithyramb-making (and most fluting and harping), taken as a whole, are really not Makings but Imitations. They differ in three points; they imitate (a) different objects, (b) by different means, (c) differently (i.e. different manner).

Some artists imitate (i.e. depict) by shapes and colors. (Obs. sometimes by art, sometimes by habit.) Some by voice. Similarly the above arts all imitate by rhythm, language, and tune, and these either (1) separate or (2) mixed.

Rhythm and tune alone, harping, fluting, and other arts with same effect—e.g. panpipes.

Rhythm without tune: dancing. (Dancers imitate characters, emotions, and experiences by means of rhythms expressed in form.)

Language alone (whether prose or verse, and one form of verse or many): this art has no name up to the present (i.e. there is no name to cover mimes and dialogues and any similar imitation made in iambics, elegiacs, &c. Commonly people attach the 'making' to the metre and say 'elegiac-makers', 'hexameter-makers,' giving them a common class-name by their metre, as if it was not their imitation that makes them 'makers').

Such an experiment would doubtless be a little absurd, but it would give an English reader some help in understanding both Aristotle's style and his meaning.

For example, their enlightenment in the literal phrase, 'how the myths ought to be put together.' The higher Greek poetry did not make up fictitious plots; its business was to express the heroic saga, the myths. Again, the literal translation of poetes, poet, as 'maker', helps to explain a term that otherwise seems a puzzle in the Poetics. If we wonder why Aristotle, and Plato before him, should lay such stress on the theory that art is imitation, it is a help to realize that common language called it 'making', and it was clearly not 'making' in the ordinary sense. The poet who was 'maker' of a Fall of Troy clearly did not make the real Fall of Troy. He made an imitation Fall of Troy. An artist who 'painted Pericles' really 'made an imitation Pericles by means of shapes and colors'. Hence we get started upon a theory of art which, whether finally satisfactory or not, is of immense importance, and are saved from the error of complaining that Aristotle did not understand the 'creative power' of art.

As a rule, no doubt, the difficulty, even though merely verbal, lies beyond the reach of so simple a tool as literal translation. To say that tragedy 'imitates good men' while comedy 'imitates bad men' strikes a modern reader as almost meaningless. The truth is that neither 'good' nor 'bad' is an exact equivalent of the Greek. It would be nearer perhaps to say that, relatively speaking, you look up to the characters of tragedy, and down upon those of comedy. High or low, serious or trivial, many other pairs of words would have to be called in, in order to cover the wide range of the common Greek words. And the point is important, because we have to consider whether in Chapter VI Aristotle really lays it down that tragedy, so far from being the story of un-happiness that we think it, is properly an imitation of eudaimonia—a word often translated 'happiness', but meaning something more like 'high life' or 'blessedness'. ²

Another difficult word which constantly recurs in the Poetics is prattein or praxis, generally translated 'to act' or 'action'. But prattein, like our 'do', also has an intransitive meaning 'to fare' either well or ill; and Professor Margoliouth has pointed out that it seems more true to say that tragedy shows how men 'fare' than how they 'act'. It shows their experiences or fortunes rather than merely their deeds. But one must not draw the line too bluntly. I should doubt whether a classical Greek writer was ordinarily conscious of the distinction between the two meanings. Certainly it is easier to regard happiness as a way of faring than as a form of action. Yet Aristotle can use the passive of prattein for things 'done' or 'gone through' (e.g. 52a, 22, 29: 55a, 25).

The fact is that much misunderstanding is often caused by our modern attempts to limit too strictly the meaning of a Greek word. Greek was very much a live language, and a language still unconscious of grammar, not, like ours, dominated by definitions and trained upon dictionaries. An instance is provided by Aristotle's famous saying that the typical tragic hero is one who falls from high state or fame, not through vice or depravity,

---

² See Margoliouth, p. 121. By water, with most editors, emends the text.

but by some great hamartia. Hamartia means originally a 'bad shot' or 'error', but is currently used for 'offence' or 'sin'. Aristotle clearly means that the typical hero is a great man with 'something wrong' in his life or character; but I think it is a mistake of method to argue whether he means 'an intellectual error' or 'a moral flaw'. The word is not so precise.

Similarly, when Aristotle says that a deed of strife or disaster is more tragic when it occurs 'amid affections' or 'among people who love each other', no doubt the phrase, as Aristotle's own examples show, would primarily suggest to a Greek feuds between near relations. Yet some of the meaning is lost if one translates simply 'within the family'.

There is another series of obscurities or confusions in the Poetics which, unless I am mistaken, arises from the fact that Aristotle was writing at a time when the great age of Greek tragedy was long past, and was using language formed in previous generations. The words and phrases remained in the tradition, but the forms of art and activity which they denoted had sometimes changed in the interval. If we date the Poetics about the year 330 B.C., as seems probable, that is more than two hundred years after the first tragedy of Thespis was produced in Athens, and more than seventy after the death of the last great masters of the tragic stage. When we remember that a training in music and poetry formed a prominent part of the education of every wellborn Athenian, we cannot be surprised at finding in Aristotle, and to a less extent in Plato, considerable traces of a tradition of technical language and even of aesthetic theory.

It is doubtless one of Aristotle's great services that he conceived so clearly the truth that literature is a thing that grows and has a history. But no writer, certainly no ancient writer, is always vigilant. Sometimes Aristotle analyses his terms, but very often he takes them for granted; and in the latter case, I think, he is sometimes deceived by them. Thus there seem to be cases where he has been affected in his conceptions of fifth-century tragedy by the practice of his own day, when the only living form of drama was the New Comedy.

For example, as we have noticed above, true Tragedy had always taken its material from the sacred myths, or heroic sagas, which to the classical Greek constituted history. But the New Comedy was in the habit of inventing its plots. Consequently Aristotle falls into using the word mythos practically in the sense of 'plot', and writing otherwise in a way that is unsuited to the tragedy of the fifth century. He says that tragedy adheres to 'the historical names' for an aesthetic reason, because what has happened is obviously possible and therefore convincing. The real reason was that the drama and the myth were simply two different expressions of the same religious kernel (p. 44). Again, he says of the Chorus (p. 65) that it should be an integral part of the play, which is true; but he also says that it' should be regarded as one of the actors', which shows to what an extent the Chorus in his day was dead and its technique forgotten. He had lost the sense of what the Chorus was in the hands of the great masters, say in the Bacchae or the Eumenides. He mistakes, again, the use of that epiphany of a God which is frequent at the end of the single plays of Euripides, and which seems to have been equally so at the end of the trilogies of Aeschylus. Having lost the living tradition, he sees neither the ritual origin nor the dramatic value of these divine epiphanies. He thinks of the convenient gods and abstractions who sometimes spoke the prologues of the New Comedy, and imagines that the God appears in order to unravel the plot. As a matter of fact, in one play which he often quotes, the Iphigenia Taurica, the plot is actually distorted at the very end in order to give an opportunity for the epiphany.[3]

One can see the effect of the tradition also in his treatment of the terms Anagnorisis and Peripeteia, which Professor Bywater translates as 'Discovery and Peripety' and Professor Butcher as 'Recognition and Reversal of Fortune'. Aristotle assumes that these two elements are normally present in any tragedy, except those which he

---

[3] See my Euripides and his Age, pp. 221-45.

calls 'simple'; we may say, roughly, in any tragedy that really has a plot. This strikes a modern reader as a very arbitrary assumption. Reversals of Fortune of some sort are perhaps usual in any varied plot, but surely not Recognitions? The clue to the puzzle lies, it can scarcely be doubted, in the historical origin of tragedy. Tragedy, according to Greek tradition, is originally the ritual play of Dionysus, performed at his festival, and representing, as Herodotus tells us, the 'sufferings' or 'passion' of that God. We are never directly told what these 'sufferings' were which were so represented; but Herodotus remarks that he found in Egypt a ritual that was 'in almost all points the same'. [4] This was the well-known ritual of Osiris, in which the god was torn in pieces, lamented, searched for, discovered or recognized, and the mourning by a sudden Reversal turned into joy. In any tragedy which still retained the stamp of its Dionysiac origin, this Discovery and Peripety might normally be expected to occur, and to occur together. I have tried to show elsewhere how many of our extant tragedies do, as a matter of fact, show the marks of this ritual. [5]

I hope it is not rash to surmise that the much-debated word *katharsis*, 'purification' or 'purgation', may have come into Aristotle's mouth from the same source. It has

---

[4] Cf. Hdt. ii. 48; cf. 42,144. The name of Dionysus must not be openly mentioned in connection with mourning (ib. 61, 132, 86). This may help to explain the transference of the tragic shows to other heroes.

[5] In Miss Harrison's Themis, pp. 341-63.

all the appearance of being an old word which is accepted and re-interpreted by Aristotle rather than a word freely chosen by him to denote the exact phenomenon he wishes to describe. At any rate the Dionysus ritual itself was a katharmos or katharsis—a purification of the community from the taints and poisons of the past year, the old contagion of sin and death. And the words of Aristotle's definition of tragedy in Chapter VI might have been used in the days of Thespis in a much cruder and less metaphorical sense. According to primitive ideas, the mimic representation on the stage of 'incidents arousing pity and fear' did act as a katharsis of such 'passions' or 'sufferings' in real life. (For the word pathemata means 'sufferings' as well as 'passions'.) It is worth remembering that in the year 361 B.C., during Aristotle's lifetime, Greek tragedies were introduced into Rome, not on artistic but on superstitious grounds, as a katharmos against a pestilence (Livy vii. 2). One cannot but suspect that in his account of the purpose of tragedy Aristotle may be using an old traditional formula, and consciously or unconsciously investing it with a new meaning, much as he has done with the word mythos.

Apart from these historical causes of misunderstanding, a good teacher who uses this book with a class will hardly fail to point out numerous points on which two equally good Greek scholars may well differ in the mere interpretation of the words. What, for instance, are the 'two natural causes' in Chapter IV which have given birth to Poetry? Are they, as our translator takes them, (1) that man is imitative, and (2) that people delight in imitations? Or are they (1) that man is imitative and people delight in imitations, and (2) the instinct for rhythm, as Professor Butcher prefers? Is it a 'creature' a thousand miles long, or a 'picture' a thousand miles long which raises some trouble in Chapter VII? The word zoon means equally 'picture' and 'animal'. Did the older poets make their characters speak like 'statesmen', politikoi, or merely like ordinary citizens, politai, while the moderns made theirs like 'professors of rhetoric'? (Chapter VI, p. 38; cf. Margoliouth's note and glossary).

It may seem as if the large uncertainties which we have indicated detract in a ruinous manner from the value of the Poetics to us as a work of criticism. Certainly if any young writer took this book as a manual of rules by which to 'commence poet', he would find himself embarrassed. But, if the book is properly read, not as a dogmatic text-book but as a first attempt, made by a man of astounding genius, to build up in the region of creative art a rational order like that which he established in logic, rhetoric, ethics, politics, physics, psychology, and almost every department of knowledge that existed in his day, then the uncertainties become rather a help than a discouragement. They give us occasion to think and use our imagination. They make us, to the best of our powers, try really to follow and criticize closely the bold gropings of an extraordinary thinker; and it is in this process, and not in any mere collection of dogmatic results, that we shall find the true value and beauty of the Poetics.

The book is of permanent value as a mere intellectual achievement; as a store of information about Greek literature; and as an original or first-hand statement of what we may call the classical view of artistic criticism. It does not regard poetry as a matter of unanalysed inspiration; it makes no concession to personal whims or fashion or ennui. It tries by rational methods to find out what is good in art and what makes it good, accepting the belief that there is just as truly a good way, and many bad ways, in poetry as in morals or in playing billiards. This is no place to try to sum up its main conclusions. But it is characteristic of the classical view that Aristotle lays his greatest stress, first, on the need for Unity in the work of art, the need that each part should subserve the whole, while irrelevancies, however brilliant in themselves, should be cast away; and next, on the demand that great art must have for its subject the great way of living. These judgements have often been misunderstood, but the truth in them is profound and goes near to the heart of things.

Characteristic, too, is the observation that different kinds of art grow and develop, but not indefinitely; they develop until they 'attain their natural form'; also the rule that each form of art should produce 'not every sort of pleasure but its proper pleasure'; and the sober language in which Aristotle, instead of speaking about the sequence of events in a tragedy being 'inevitable', as we bombastic moderns do, merely recommends that they should be 'either necessary or probable' and 'appear to happen because of one another'.

Conceptions and attitudes of mind such as these constitute what we may call the classical faith in matters of art and poetry; a faith which is never perhaps fully accepted in any age, yet, unlike others, is never forgotten but lives by being constantly criticized, re-asserted, and rebelled against. For the fashions of the ages vary in this direction and that, but they vary for the most part from a central road which was struck out by the imagination of Greece.

G. M

Aristotle on the Art of Poetry

1

Our subject being Poetry, I propose to speak not only of the art in general but also of its species and their respective capacities; of the structure of plot required for a good poem; of the number and nature of the constituent parts of a poem; and likewise of any other matters in the same line of inquiry. Let us follow the natural order and begin with the primary facts.

Epic poetry and Tragedy, as also Comedy, Dithyrambic poetry, and most flute-playing and lyre-playing, are all, viewed as a whole, modes of imitation. But at the same time they differ from one another in three ways, either by a difference of kind in their means, or by differences in the objects, or in the manner of their imitations.

I. Just as form and color are used as means by some, who (whether by art or constant practice) imitate and portray many things by their aid, and the voice is used by others; so also in the above-mentioned group of arts, the means with them as a whole are rhythm, language, and harmony—used, however, either singly or in certain combinations. A combination of rhythm and harmony alone is the means in flute-playing and lyre-playing, and any other arts there may be of the same description, e.g. imitative piping. Rhythm alone, without harmony, is the means in the dancer's imitations; for even he, by the rhythms of his attitudes, may represent men's characters, as well as what they do and suffer. There is further an art which imitates by language alone, without harmony, in prose or in verse, and if in verse, either in some one or in a plurality of metres. This form of imitation is to this day without a name. We have no common name for a mime of Sophron or Xenarchus and a Socratic Conversation; and we should still be without one even if the imitation in the two instances were in trimeters or elegiacs or some other kind of verse—though it is the way with people to tack on 'poet' to the name of a metre, and talk of elegiac-poets and epic-poets, thinking that they call them poets not by reason of the imitative nature of their work, but indiscriminately by reason of the metre they write in. Even if a theory of medicine or physical philosophy be put forth in a metrical form, it is usual to describe the writer in this way; Homer and Empedocles, however, have really nothing in common apart from their metre; so that, if the one is to be called a poet, the other should be termed a physicist rather than a poet. We should be in the same position also, if the imitation in these instances were in all the metres, like the Centaur (a rhapsody in a medley of all metres) of Chaeremon; and Chaeremon one has to recognize as a poet. So much, then, as to these arts. There are, lastly, certain other arts, which combine all the means enumerated, rhythm, melody, and verse, e.g. Dithyrambic and Nomic poetry, Tragedy and Comedy; with this difference, however, that the three kinds of means are in some of them all employed together, and in others brought in separately, one after the other. These elements of difference in the above arts I term the means of their imitation.

2

II. The objects the imitator represents are actions, with agents who are necessarily either good men or bad—the diversities of human character being nearly always derivative from this primary distinction, since the line between virtue and vice is one dividing the whole of mankind. It follows, therefore, that the agents represented must be either above our own level of goodness, or beneath it, or just such as we are in the same way as, with the painters, the personages of Polygnotus are better than we are, those of Pauson worse, and those of Dionysius just like ourselves. It is clear that each of the above-mentioned arts will admit of these differences, and that it will become a separate art by representing objects with this point of difference. Even in dancing, flute-playing, and lyre-playing such diversities are possible; and they are also possible in the nameless art that uses language, prose or verse without harmony, as its means; Homer's personages, for instance, are better than we are; Cleophon's are on our own level; and those of Hegemon of Thasos, the first writer of parodies, and Nicochares, the author of the Diliad, are beneath it. The same is true of the Dithyramb and the Nome: the personages may be presented in them with the difference exemplified in the... of... and Argas, and in the Cyclopses of Timotheus and Philoxenus. This difference it is that distinguishes Tragedy and Comedy also; the one would make its personages worse, and the other better, than the men of the present day.

III. A third difference in these arts is in the manner in which each kind of object is represented. Given both the same means and the same kind of object for imitation, one may either (1) speak at one moment in narrative and at another in an assumed character, as Homer does; or (2) one may remain the same throughout, without any such change; or (3) the imitators may represent the whole story dramatically, as though they were actually doing the things described.

As we said at the beginning, therefore, the differences in the imitation of these arts come under three heads, their means, their objects, and their manner.

So that as an imitator Sophocles will be on one side akin to Homer, both portraying good men; and on another to Aristophanes, since both present their personages as acting and doing. This in fact, according to some, is the reason for plays being termed dramas, because in a play the personages act the story. Hence too both Tragedy and Comedy are claimed by the Dorians as their discoveries; Comedy by the Megarians—by those in Greece as having arisen when Megara became a democracy, and by the Sicilian Megarians on the ground that the poet Epicharmus was of their country, and a good deal earlier than Chionides and Magnes; even Tragedy also is claimed by certain of the Peloponnesian Dorians. In support of this claim they point to the words 'comedy' and 'drama'. Their word for the outlying hamlets, they say, is comae, whereas Athenians call them demes—thus assuming that comedians got the name not from their comoe or revels, but from their strolling from hamlet to hamlet, lack of appreciation keeping them out of the city.

Their word also for 'to act', they say, is dran, whereas Athenians use prattein.

So much, then, as to the number and nature of the points of difference in the imitation of these arts.

4

It is clear that the general origin of poetry was due to two causes, each of them part of human nature. Imitation is natural to man from childhood, one of his advantages over the lower animals being this, that he is the most imitative creature in the world, and learns at first by imitation. And it is also natural for all to delight in works of imitation. The truth of this second point is shown by experience: though the objects themselves may be painful to see, we delight to view the most realistic representations of them in art, the forms for example of the lowest animals and of dead bodies. The explanation is to be found in a further fact: to be learning something is the greatest of pleasures not only to the philosopher but also to the rest of mankind, however small their capacity for it; the reason of the delight in seeing the picture is that one is at the same time learning — gathering the meaning of things, e.g. that the man there is so-and-so; for if one has not seen the thing before, one's pleasure will not be in the picture as an imitation of it, but will be due to the execution or coloring or some similar cause. Imitation, then, being natural to us—as also the sense of harmony and rhythm, the metres being obviously species of rhythms—it was through their original aptitude, and by a series of improvements for the most part gradual on their first efforts, that they created poetry out of their improvisations.

Poetry, however, soon broke up into two kinds according to the differences of character in the individual poets; for the graver among them would represent noble actions, and those of noble personages; and the meaner sort the actions of the ignoble. The latter class produced invectives at first, just as others did hymns and panegyrics. We know of no such poem by any of the pre-Homeric poets, though there were probably many such writers among them; instances, however, may be found from Homer downwards, e.g. his Margites, and the similar poems of others. In this poetry of invective its natural fitness brought an iambic metre into use; hence our present term 'iambic', because it was the metre of their 'iambs' or invectives against one another. The result was that the old poets became some of them writers of heroic and others of iambic verse. Homer's position, however, is peculiar: just as he was in the serious style the poet of poets, standing alone not only through the literary excellence, but also through the dramatic character of his imitations, so too he was the first to outline for us the general forms of Comedy by producing not a dramatic invective, but a dramatic picture of the Ridiculous; his Margites in fact stands in the same relation to our comedies as the Iliad and Odyssey to our tragedies. As soon, however, as Tragedy and Comedy appeared in the field, those naturally drawn to the one line of poetry became writers of comedies instead of iambs, and those naturally drawn to the other, writers of tragedies instead of epics, because these new modes of art were grander and of more esteem than the old.

If it be asked whether Tragedy is now all that it need be in its formative elements, to consider that, and decide it theoretically and in relation to the theatres, is a matter for another inquiry.

It certainly began in improvisations—as did also Comedy; the one originating with the authors of the Dithyramb, the other with those of the phallic songs, which still survive as institutions in many of our cities. And its advance after that was little by little, through their improving on whatever they had before them at each stage. It was in fact only after a long series of changes that the movement of Tragedy stopped on its attaining to its natural form. (1) The number of actors was first increased to two by Aeschylus, who curtailed the business of the Chorus, and made the dialogue, or spoken portion, take the leading part in the play. (2) A third actor and scenery were due to Sophocles. (3) Tragedy acquired also its magnitude. Discarding short stories and a ludicrous diction, through its passing out of its satiric stage, it assumed, though only at a late point in its progress, a tone of dignity; and its metre changed then from trochaic to iambic. The reason for their original use of the trochaic tetrameter was that their poetry was satiric and more connected with dancing than it now is. As soon, however, as a spoken part came in, nature herself found the appropriate metre. The iambic, we know, is the most speakable of metres, as is shown by the fact that we very often fall into it in conversation, whereas we rarely talk hexameters, and only when we depart from the speaking tone of voice. (4) Another change was a plurality of episodes or acts. As for the remaining matters, the superadded embellishments and the account of their introduction, these must be taken as said, as it would probably be a long piece of work to go through the details.

5

As for Comedy, it is (as has been observed) an imitation of men worse than the average; worse, however, not as regards any and every sort of fault, but only as regards one particular kind, the Ridiculous, which is a species of the Ugly. The Ridiculous may be defined as a mistake or deformity not productive of pain or harm to others; the mask, for instance, that excites laughter, is something ugly and distorted without causing pain.

Though the successive changes in Tragedy and their authors are not unknown, we cannot say the same of Comedy; its early stages passed unnoticed, because it was not as yet taken up in a serious way. It was only at a late point in its progress that a chorus of comedians was officially granted by the archon; they used to be mere volunteers. It had also already certain definite forms at the time when the record of those termed comic poets begins. Who it was who supplied it with masks, or prologues, or a plurality of actors and the like, has remained unknown. The invented Fable, or Plot, however, originated in Sicily, with Epicharmus and Phormis; of Athenian poets Crates was the first to drop the Comedy of invective and frame stories of a general and non-personal nature, in other words, Fables or Plots.

Epic poetry, then, has been seen to agree with Tragedy to this extent, that of being an imitation of serious subjects in a grand kind of verse. It differs from it, however, (1) in that it is in one kind of verse and in narrative form; and (2) in its length—which is due to its action having no fixed limit of time, whereas Tragedy endeavors to keep as far as possible within a single circuit of the sun, or something near that. This, I say, is another point of difference between them, though at first the practice in this respect was just the same in tragedies as in epic poems. They differ also (3) in their constituents, some being common to both and others peculiar to Tragedy— hence a judge of good and bad in Tragedy is a judge of that in epic poetry also. All the parts of an epic are included in Tragedy; but those of Tragedy are not all of them to be found in the Epic.

6

Reserving hexameter poetry and Comedy for consideration hereafter, let us proceed now to the discussion of Tragedy; before doing so, however, we must gather up the definition resulting from what has been said. A tragedy, then, is the imitation of an action that is serious and also, as having magnitude, complete in itself; in language with pleasurable accessories, each kind brought in separately in the parts of the work; in a dramatic, not in a narrative form; with incidents arousing pity and fear, wherewith to accomplish its catharsis of such emotions. Here by 'language with pleasurable accessories' I mean that with rhythm and harmony or song superadded; and by 'the kinds separately' I mean that some portions are worked out with verse only, and others in turn with song.

I. As they act the stories, it follows that in the first place the Spectacle (or stage-appearance of the actors) must be some part of the whole; and in the second Melody and Diction, these two being the means of their imitation. Here by 'Diction' I mean merely this, the composition of the verses; and by 'Melody', what is too completely understood to require explanation. But further: the subject represented also is an action; and the action involves agents, who must necessarily have their distinctive qualities both of character and thought, since it is from these that we ascribe certain qualities to their actions. There are in the natural order of things, therefore, two causes, Character and Thought, of their actions, and consequently of their success or failure in their lives. Now the action (that which was done) is represented in the play by the Fable or Plot. The Fable, in our present sense of the term, is simply this, the combination of the incidents, or things done in the story; whereas Character is what makes us ascribe certain moral qualities to the agents; and Thought is shown in all they say when proving a particular point or, it may be, enunciating a general truth. There are six parts consequently of every tragedy, as a whole, that is, of such or such quality, viz. a Fable or Plot, Characters, Diction, Thought, Spectacle and Melody; two of them arising from the means, one from the manner, and three from the objects of the dramatic imitation; and there is nothing else besides these six. Of these, its formative elements, then, not a few of the dramatists have made due use, as every play, one may say, admits of Spectacle, Character, Fable, Diction, Melody, and Thought.

II. The most important of the six is the combination of the incidents of the story.

Tragedy is essentially an imitation not of persons but of action and life, of happiness and misery. All human happiness or misery takes the form of action; the end for which we live is a certain kind of activity, not a quality. Character gives us qualities, but it is in our actions—what we do—that we are happy or the reverse. In a play accordingly they do not act in order to portray the Characters; they include the Characters for the sake of the action. So that it is the action in it, i.e. its Fable or Plot, that is the end and purpose of the tragedy; and the end is everywhere the chief thing. Besides this, a tragedy is impossible without action, but there may be one without Character. The tragedies of most of the moderns are characterless—a defect common among poets of all kinds, and with its counterpart in painting in Zeuxis as compared with Polygnotus; for whereas the latter is strong in character, the work of Zeuxis is devoid of it. And again: one may string together a series of characteristic speeches of the utmost finish as regards Diction and Thought, and yet fail to produce the true tragic effect; but one will have much better success with a tragedy which, however inferior in these respects, has a Plot, a combination of incidents, in it. And again: the most powerful elements of attraction in Tragedy, the Peripeties and Discoveries, are parts of the Plot. A further proof is in the fact that beginners succeed earlier with the Diction and Characters than with the construction of a story; and the same may be said of nearly all the early dramatists. We maintain, therefore, that the first essential, the life and soul, so to speak, of Tragedy is the Plot; and that the Characters come second—compare the parallel in painting, where the most beautiful colors laid on without order will not give one the same pleasure as a simple black-and-white sketch of a portrait. We maintain that Tragedy is primarily an imitation of action, and that it is mainly for the sake of the action that it imitates the personal agents. Third comes the element of Thought, i.e. the power of saying whatever can be said, or what is appropriate to the occasion. This is what, in the speeches in Tragedy, falls under the arts of Politics and Rhetoric; for the older poets make their personages discourse like statesmen, and the moderns like rhetoricians. One must not confuse it with Character. Character in a play is that which reveals the moral purpose of the agents, i.e. the sort of thing they seek or avoid, where that is not obvious—hence there is no room for Character in a speech on a purely indifferent subject. Thought, on the other hand, is shown in all they say when proving or disproving some particular point, or enunciating some universal proposition. Fourth among the literary elements is the Diction of the personages, i.e. as before explained, the expression of their thoughts in words, which is practically the same thing with verse as with prose. As for the two remaining parts, the Melody is the greatest of the pleasurable accessories of Tragedy. The Spectacle, though an attraction, is the least artistic of all the parts, and has least to do with the art of poetry. The tragic effect is quite possible without a public performance and actors; and besides, the getting-up of the Spectacle is more a matter for the costumier than the poet.

7

Having thus distinguished the parts, let us now consider the proper construction of the Fable or Plot, as that is at once the first and the most important thing in Tragedy. We have laid it down that a tragedy is an imitation of an action that is complete in itself, as a whole of some magnitude; for a whole may be of no magnitude to speak of. Now a whole is that which has beginning, middle, and end. A beginning is that which is not itself necessarily after anything else, and which has naturally something else after it; an end is that which is naturally after something itself, either as its necessary or usual consequent, and with nothing else after it; and a middle, that which is by nature after one thing and has also another after it. A well-constructed Plot, therefore, cannot either begin or end at any point one likes; beginning and end in it must be of the forms just described. Again: to be beautiful, a living creature, and every whole made up of parts, must not only present a certain order in its arrangement of parts, but also be of a certain definite magnitude. Beauty is a matter of size and order, and therefore impossible either (1) in a very minute creature, since our perception becomes indistinct as it approaches instantaneity; or (2) in a creature of vast size—one, say, 1,000 miles long—as in that case, instead of the object being seen all at once, the unity and wholeness of it is lost to the beholder.

Just in the same way, then, as a beautiful whole made up of parts, or a beautiful living creature, must be of some size, a size to be taken in by the eye, so a story or Plot must be of some length, but of a length to be taken in by the memory. As for the limit of its length, so far as that is relative to public performances and spectators, it does not fall within the theory of poetry. If they had to perform a hundred tragedies, they would be timed by water-clocks, as they are said to have been at one period. The limit, however, set by the actual nature of the thing is this: the longer the story, consistently with its being comprehensible as a whole, the finer it is by reason of its magnitude. As a rough general formula, 'a length which allows of the hero passing by a series of probable or necessary stages from misfortune to happiness, or from happiness to misfortune', may suffice as a limit for the magnitude of the story.

8

The Unity of a Plot does not consist, as some suppose, in its having one man as its subject. An infinity of things befall that one man, some of which it is impossible to reduce to unity; and in like manner there are many actions of one man which cannot be made to form one action. One sees, therefore, the mistake of all the poets who have written a Heracleid, a Theseid, or similar poems; they suppose that, because Heracles was one man, the story also of Heracles must be one story. Homer, however, evidently understood this point quite well, whether by art or instinct, just in the same way as he excels the rest in every other respect. In writing an Odyssey, he did not make the poem cover all that ever befell his hero—it befell him, for instance, to get wounded on Parnassus and also to feign madness at the time of the call to arms, but the two incidents had no probable or necessary connection with one another—instead of doing that, he took an action with a Unity of the kind we are describing as the subject of the Odyssey, as also of the Iliad. The truth is that, just as in the other imitative arts one imitation is always of one thing, so in poetry the story, as an imitation of action, must represent one action, a complete whole, with its several incidents so closely connected that the transposal or withdrawal of any one of them will disjoin and dislocate the whole. For that which makes no perceptible difference by its presence or absence is no real part of the whole.

9

From what we have said it will be seen that the poet's function is to describe, not the thing that has happened, but a kind of thing that might happen, i.e. what is possible as being probable or necessary. The distinction between historian and poet is not in the one writing prose and the other verse—you might put the work of

Herodotus into verse, and it would still be a species of history; it consists really in this, that the one describes the thing that has been, and the other a kind of thing that might be. Hence poetry is something more philosophic and of graver import than history, since its statements are of the nature rather of universals, whereas those of history are singulars. By a universal statement I mean one as to what such or such a kind of man will probably or necessarily say or do—which is the aim of poetry, though it affixes proper names to the characters; by a singular statement, one as to what, say, Alcibiades did or had done to him. In Comedy this has become clear by this time; it is only when their plot is already made up of probable incidents that they give it a basis of proper names, choosing for the purpose any names that may occur to them, instead of writing like the old iambic poets about particular persons. In Tragedy, however, they still adhere to the historic names; and for this reason: what convinces is the possible; now whereas we are not yet sure as to the possibility of that which has not happened, that which has happened is manifestly possible, else it would not have come to pass. Nevertheless even in Tragedy there are some plays with but one or two known names in them, the rest being inventions; and there are some without a single known name, e.g. Agathon's Anthens, in which both incidents and names are of the poet's invention; and it is no less delightful on that account. So that one must not aim at a rigid adherence to the traditional stories on which tragedies are based. It would be absurd, in fact, to do so, as even the known stories are only known to a few, though they are a delight none the less to all.

It is evident from the above that, the poet must be more the poet of his stories or Plots than of his verses, inasmuch as he is a poet by virtue of the imitative element in his work, and it is actions that he imitates. And if he should come to take a subject from actual history, he is none the less a poet for that; since some historic occurrences may very well be in the probable and possible order of things; and it is in that aspect of them that he is their poet.

Of simple Plots and actions the episodic are the worst. I call a Plot episodic when there is neither probability nor necessity in the sequence of episodes. Actions of this sort bad poets construct through their own fault, and good ones on account of the players. His work being for public performance, a good poet often stretches out a Plot beyond its capabilities, and is thus obliged to twist the sequence of incident.

Tragedy, however, is an imitation not only of a complete action, but also of incidents arousing pity and fear. Such incidents have the very greatest effect on the mind when they occur unexpectedly and at the same time in consequence of one another; there is more of the marvelous in them then than if they happened of themselves or by mere chance. Even matters of chance seem most marvelous if there is an appearance of design as it were in them; as for instance the statue of Mitys at Argos killed the author of Mitys' death by falling down on him when a looker-on at a public spectacle; for incidents like that we think to be not without a meaning. A Plot, therefore, of this sort is necessarily finer than others.

10

Plots are either simple or complex, since the actions they represent are naturally of this twofold description. The action, proceeding in the way defined, as one continuous whole, I call simple, when the change in the hero's fortunes takes place without Peripety or Discovery; and complex, when it involves one or the other, or both. These should each of them arise out of the structure of the Plot itself, so as to be the consequence, necessary or probable, of the antecedents. There is a great difference between a thing happening propter hoc and post hoc.

11

A Peripety is the change from one state of things within the play to its opposite of the kind described, and that too in the way we are saying, in the probable or necessary sequence of events; as it is for instance in Oedipus: here the opposite state of things is produced by the Messenger, who, coming to gladden Oedipus and to remove his fears as to his mother, reveals the secret of his birth. And in Lynceus: just as he is being led off for execution, with Danaus at his side to put him to death, the incidents preceding this bring it about that he is saved and Danaus put to death. A Discovery is, as the very word implies, a change from ignorance to knowledge, and thus to either love or hate, in the personages marked for good or evil fortune. The finest form of Discovery is one attended by Peripeties, like that which goes with the Discovery in Oedipus. There are no doubt other forms of it; what we have said may happen in a way in reference to inanimate things, even things of a very casual kind; and it is also possible to discover whether someone has done or not done something. But the form most directly connected with the Plot and the action of the piece is the first-mentioned. This, with a Peripety, will arouse either pity or fear—actions of that nature being what Tragedy is assumed to represent; and it will also serve to bring about the happy or unhappy ending. The Discovery, then, being of persons, it may be that of one party only to the other, the latter being already known; or both the parties may have to discover themselves. Iphigenia, for instance, was discovered to Orestes by sending the letter; and another Discovery was required to reveal him to Iphigenia.

Two parts of the Plot, then, Peripety and Discovery, are on matters of this sort. A third part is Suffering; which we may define as an action of a destructive or painful nature, such as murders on the stage, tortures, woundings, and the like. The other two have been already explained.

12

The parts of Tragedy to be treated as formative elements in the whole were mentioned in a previous Chapter. From the point of view, however, of its quantity, i.e. the separate sections into which it is divided, a tragedy has the following parts: Prologue, Episode, Exode, and a choral portion, distinguished into Parode and Stasimon; these two are common to all tragedies, whereas songs from the stage and Commoe are only found in some. The Prologue is all that precedes the Parode of the chorus; an Episode all that comes in between two whole choral songs; the Exode all that follows after the last choral song. In the choral portion the Parode is the whole first statement of the chorus; a Stasimon, a song of the chorus without anapaests or trochees; a Commas, a lamentation sung by chorus and actor in concert. The parts of Tragedy to be used as formative elements in the whole we have already mentioned; the above are its parts from the point of view of its quantity, or the separate sections into which it is divided.

13

The next points after what we have said above will be these: (1) What is the poet to aim at, and what is he to avoid, in constructing his Plots? and (2) What are the conditions on which the tragic effect depends?

We assume that, for the finest form of Tragedy, the Plot must be not simple but complex; and further, that it must imitate actions arousing pity and fear, since that is the distinctive function of this kind of imitation. It follows, therefore, that there are three forms of Plot to be avoided. (1) A good man must not be seen passing from happiness to misery, or (2) a bad man from misery to happiness.

The first situation is not fear-inspiring or piteous, but simply odious to us. The second is the most untragic that can be; it has no one of the requisites of Tragedy; it does not appeal either to the human feeling in us, or to our pity, or to our fears. Nor, on the other hand, should (3) an extremely bad man be seen falling from happiness into misery. Such a story may arouse the human feeling in us, but it will not move us to either pity or fear; pity is occasioned by undeserved misfortune, and fear by that of one like ourselves; so that there will be nothing either piteous or fear-inspiring in the situation. There remains, then, the intermediate kind of personage, a man not pre-eminently virtuous and just, whose misfortune, however, is brought upon him not by vice and depravity but by some error of judgment, of the number of those in the enjoyment of great reputation and prosperity; e.g. Oedipus, Thyestes, and the men of note of similar families. The perfect Plot, accordingly, must have a single, and not (as some tell us) a double issue; the change in the hero's fortunes must be not from misery to happiness, but on the contrary from happiness to misery; and the cause of it must lie not in any depravity, but in some great error on his part; the man himself being either such as we have described, or better, not worse, than that. Fact also confirms our theory. Though the poets began by accepting any tragic story that came to hand, in these days the finest tragedies are always on the story of some few houses, on that of Alemeon, Oedipus, Orestes,

Meleager, Thyestes, Telephus, or any others that may have been involved, as either agents or sufferers, in some deed of horror. The theoretically best tragedy, then, has a Plot of this description. The critics, therefore, are wrong who blame Euripides for taking this line in his tragedies, and giving many of them an unhappy ending. It is, as we have said, the right line to take. The best proof is this: on the stage, and in the public performances, such plays, properly worked out, are seen to be the most truly tragic; and Euripides, even if his elecution be faulty in every other point, is seen to be nevertheless the most tragic certainly of the dramatists. After this comes the construction of Plot which some rank first, one with a double story (like the Odyssey) and an opposite issue for the good and the bad personages. It is ranked as first only through the weakness of the audiences; the poets merely follow their public, writing as its wishes dictate. But the pleasure here is not that of Tragedy. It belongs rather to Comedy, where the bitterest enemies in the piece (e.g. Orestes and Aegisthus) walk off good friends at the end, with no slaying of any one by any one.

14

The tragic fear and pity may be aroused by the Spectacle; but they may also be aroused by the very structure and incidents of the play—which is the better way and shows the better poet. The Plot in fact should be so framed that, even without seeing the things take place, he who simply hears the account of them shall be filled with horror and pity at the incidents; which is just the effect that the mere recital of the story in Oedipus would have on one. To produce this same effect by means of the Spectacle is less artistic, and requires extraneous aid. Those, however, who make use of the Spectacle to put before us that which is merely monstrous and not productive of fear, are wholly out of touch with Tragedy; not every kind of pleasure should be required of a tragedy, but only its own proper pleasure.

The tragic pleasure is that of pity and fear, and the poet has to produce it by a work of imitation; it is clear, therefore, that the causes should be included in the incidents of his story. Let us see, then, what kinds of incident strike one as horrible, or rather as piteous. In a deed of this description the parties must necessarily be either friends, or enemies, or indifferent to one another. Now when enemy does it on enemy, there is nothing to move us to pity either in his doing or in his meditating the deed, except so far as the actual pain of the sufferer is concerned; and the same is true when the parties are indifferent to one another. Whenever the tragic deed, however, is done within the family—when murder or the like is done or meditated by brother on brother, by son on father, by mother on son, or son on mother—these are the situations the poet should seek after. The traditional stories, accordingly, must be kept as they are, e.g. the murder of Clytaemnestra by Orestes and of Eriphyle by Alcmeon. At the same time even with these there is something left to the poet himself; it is for him to devise the right way of treating them. Let us explain more clearly what we mean by 'the right way'. The deed of horror may be done by the doer knowingly and consciously, as in the old poets, and in Medea's murder of her children in Euripides. Or he may do it, but in ignorance of his relationship, and discover that afterwards, as does the Oedipus in Sophocles. Here the deed is outside the play; but it may be within it, like the act of the Alcmeon in Astydamas, or that of the Telegonus in Ulysses Wounded. A third possibility is for one meditating some deadly injury to another, in ignorance of his relationship, to make the discovery in time to draw back. These exhaust the possibilities, since the deed must necessarily be either done or not done, and either knowingly or unknowingly.

The worst situation is when the personage is with full knowledge on the point of doing the deed, and leaves it undone. It is odious and also (through the absence of suffering) untragic; hence it is that no one is made to act thus except in some few instances, e.g. Haemon and Creon in Antigone. Next after this comes the actual perpetration of the deed meditated. A better situation than that, however, is for the deed to be done in ignorance, and the relationship discovered afterwards, since there is nothing odious in it, and the Discovery will serve to astound us. But the best of all is the last; what we have in Cresphontes, for example, where Merope, on the point of slaying her son, recognizes him in time; in Iphigenia, where sister and brother are in a like position; and in Helle, where the son recognizes his mother, when on the point of giving her up to her enemy.

This will explain why our tragedies are restricted (as we said just now) to such a small number of families. It was accident rather than art that led the poets in quest of subjects to embody this kind of incident in their Plots. They are still obliged, accordingly, to have recourse to the families in which such horrors have occurred.

On the construction of the Plot, and the kind of Plot required for Tragedy, enough has now been said.

15

In the Characters there are four points to aim at. First and foremost, that they shall be good. There will be an element of character in the play, if (as has been observed) what a personage says or does reveals a certain moral purpose; and a good element of character, if the purpose so revealed is good. Such goodness is possible in every type of personage, even in a woman or a slave, though the one is perhaps an inferior, and the other a wholly worthless being. The second point is to make them appropriate. The Character before us may be, say, manly; but it is not appropriate in a female Character to be manly, or clever. The third is to make them like the reality, which is not the same as their being good and appropriate, in our sense of the term. The fourth is to make them consistent and the same throughout; even if inconsistency be part of the man before one for imitation as presenting that form of character, he should still be consistently inconsistent. We have an instance of baseness of character, not required for the story, in the Menelaus in Orestes; of the incongruous and unbefitting in the lamentation of Ulysses in Scylla, and in the (clever) speech of Melanippe; and of inconsistency in Iphigenia at Aulis, where Iphigenia the suppliant is utterly unlike the later Iphigenia. The right thing, however, is in the Characters just as in the incidents of the play to endeavor always after the necessary or the probable; so that whenever such-and-such a personage says or does such-and-such a thing, it shall be the probable or necessary outcome of his character; and whenever this incident follows on that, it shall be either the necessary or the probable consequence of it. From this one sees (to digress for a moment) that the Denouement also should arise out of the plot itself, arid not depend on a stage-artifice, as in Medea, or in the story of the (arrested) departure of the Greeks in the Iliad. The artifice must be reserved for matters outside the play—for past events beyond human knowledge, or events yet to come, which require to be foretold or announced; since it is the privilege of the Gods to know everything. There should be nothing improbable among the actual incidents. If it be unavoidable, however, it should be outside the tragedy, like the improbability in the Oedipus of Sophocles. But to return to the Characters. As Tragedy is an imitation of personages better than the ordinary man, we in our way should follow the example of good portrait-painters, who reproduce the distinctive features of a man, and at the same time, without losing the likeness, make him handsomer than he is. The poet in like manner, in portraying men quick or slow to anger, or with similar infirmities of character, must know how to represent them as such, and at the same time as good men, as Agathon and Homer have represented Achilles.

All these rules one must keep in mind throughout, and further, those also for such points of stage-effect as directly depend on the art of the poet, since in these too one may often make mistakes. Enough, however, has been said on the subject in one of our published writings.

16

Discovery in general has been explained already. As for the species of Discovery, the first to be noted is (1) the least artistic form of it, of which the poets make most use through mere lack of invention, Discovery by signs or marks. Of these signs some are congenital, like the 'lance-head which the Earth-born have on them', or 'stars', such as Carcinus brings in in his Thyestes; others acquired after birth—these latter being either marks on the body, e.g. scars, or external tokens, like necklaces, or to take another sort of instance, the ark in the Discovery in Tyro. Even these, however, admit of two uses, a better and a worse; the scar of Ulysses is an instance; the Discovery of him through it is made in one way by the nurse and in another by the swineherds. A Discovery using signs as a means of assurance is less artistic, as indeed are all such as imply reflection; whereas one bringing them in all of a sudden, as in the Bath-story, is of a better order. Next after these are (2) Discoveries made directly by the poet; which are inartistic for that very reason; e.g. Orestes' Discovery of himself in Iphigenia: whereas his sister reveals who she is by the letter, Orestes is made to say himself what the poet rather than the story demands. This, therefore, is not far removed from the first-mentioned fault, since he might have presented certain tokens as well. Another instance is the 'shuttle's voice' in the Tereus of Sophocles. (3) A third species is Discovery through memory, from a man's consciousness being awakened by something seen or heard. Thus in The Cyprioe of Dicaeogenes, the sight of the picture makes the man burst into tears; and in the Tale of Alcinous, hearing the harper Ulysses is reminded of the past and weeps; the Discovery of them being the result. (4) A fourth kind is Discovery through reasoning; e.g. in The Choephoroe: 'One like me is here; there is no one like me but Orestes; he, therefore, must be here.' Or that which Polyidus the Sophist suggested for Iphigenia; since it was natural for Orestes to reflect: 'My sister was sacrificed, and I am to be sacrificed like her.' Or that in the Tydeus of Theodectes: 'I came to find a son, and am to die myself.' Or that in The Phinidae: on seeing the place the women inferred their fate, that they were to die there, since they had also been exposed there. (5) There is, too, a composite Discovery arising from bad reasoning on the side of the other party. An instance of it is in Ulysses the False Messenger: he said he should know the bow — which he had not seen; but to suppose from that that he would know it again (as though he had once seen it) was bad reasoning. (6) The best of all Discoveries, however, is that arising from the incidents themselves, when the great surprise comes about through a probable incident, like that in the Oedipus of Sophocles; and also in Iphigenia; for it was not improbable that she should wish to have a letter taken home. These last are the only Discoveries independent of the artifice of signs and necklaces. Next after them come Discoveries through reasoning.

17

At the time when he is constructing his Plots, and engaged on the Diction in which they are worked out, the poet should remember (1) to put the actual scenes as far as possible before his eyes. In this way, seeing everything with the vividness of an eye-witness as it were, he will devise what is appropriate, and be least likely to overlook incongruities. This is shown by what was censured in Carcinus, the return of Amphiaraus from the sanctuary; it would have passed unnoticed, if it had not been actually seen by the audience; but on the stage his play failed, the incongruity of the incident offending the spectators. (2) As far as may be, too, the poet should even act his story with the very gestures of his personages. Given the same natural qualifications, he who feels the emotions to be described will be the most convincing; distress and anger, for instance, are portrayed most truthfully by one who is feeling them at the moment. Hence it is that poetry demands a man with special gift for it, or else one with a touch of madness in him; the former can easily assume the required mood, and the latter may be actually beside himself with emotion. (3) His story, again, whether already made or of his own making, he should first simplify and reduce to a universal form, before proceeding to lengthen it out by the insertion of episodes. The following will show how the universal element in Iphigenia, for instance, may be viewed: A certain maiden having been offered in sacrifice, and spirited away from her sacrifices into another land, where the custom was to sacrifice all strangers to the Goddess, she was made there the priestess of this rite. Long after that the brother of the priestess happened to come; the fact, however, of the oracle having for a certain reason bidden him go thither, and his object in going, are outside the Plot of the play. On his coming he was arrested, and about to be sacrificed, when he revealed who he was—either as Euripides puts it, or (as suggested by Polyidus) by the not improbable exclamation, 'So I too am doomed to be sacrificed, as my sister was'; and the disclosure led to his salvation. This done, the next thing, after the proper names have been fixed as a basis for the story, is to work in episodes or accessory incidents. One must mind, however, that the episodes are appropriate, like the fit of madness in Orestes, which led to his arrest, and the purifying, which brought about his salvation. In plays, then, the episodes are short; in epic poetry they serve to lengthen out the poem. The argument of the Odyssey is not a long one.

A certain man has been abroad many years; Poseidon is ever on the watch for him, and he is all alone. Matters at home too have come to this, that his substance is being wasted and his son's death plotted by suitors to his wife. Then he arrives there himself after his grievous sufferings; reveals himself, and falls on his enemies; and the end is his salvation and their death. This being all that is proper to the Odyssey, everything else in it is episode.

18

(4) There is a further point to be borne in mind. Every tragedy is in part Complication and in part Denouement; the incidents before the opening scene, and often certain also of those within the play, forming the Complication; and the rest the Denouement. By Complication I mean all from the beginning of the story to the point just before the change in the hero's fortunes; by Denouement, all from the beginning of the change to the end. In the Lynceus of Theodectes, for instance, the Complication includes, together with the presupposed incidents, the seizure of the child and that in turn of the parents; and the Denouement all from the indictment for the murder to the end. Now it is right, when one speaks of a tragedy

as the same or not the same as another, to do so on the ground before all else of their Plot, i.e. as having the same or not the same Complication and Denouement. Yet there are many dramatists who, after a good Complication, fail in the Denouement. But it is necessary for both points of construction to be always duly mastered. (5) There are four distinct species of Tragedy—that being the number of the constituents also that have been mentioned: first, the complex Tragedy, which is all Peripety and Discovery; second, the Tragedy of suffering, e.g. the Ajaxes and Ixions; third, the Tragedy of character, e.g. The Phthiotides and Peleus. The fourth constituent is that of 'Spectacle', exemplified in The Phorcides, in Prometheus, and in all plays with the scene laid in the nether world. The poet's aim, then, should be to combine every element of interest, if possible, or else the more important and the major part of them. This is now especially necessary owing to the unfair criticism to which the poet is subjected in these days. Just because there have been poets before him strong in the several species of tragedy, the critics now expect the one man to surpass that which was the strong point of each one of his predecessors. (6) One should also remember what has been said more than once, and not write a tragedy on an epic body of incident (i.e. one with a plurality of stories in it), by attempting to dramatize, for instance, the entire story of the Iliad. In the epic owing to its scale every part is treated at proper length; with a drama, however, on the same story the result is very disappointing. This is shown by the fact that all who have dramatized the fall of Ilium in its entirety, and not part by part, like Euripides, or the whole of the Niobe story, instead of a portion, like Aeschylus, either fail utterly or have but ill success on the stage; for that and that alone was enough to ruin a play by Agathon. Yet in their Peripeties, as also in their simple plots, the poets I mean show wonderful skill in aiming at the kind of effect they desire—a tragic situation that arouses the human feeling in one, like the clever villain (e.g. Sisyphus) deceived, or the brave wrongdoer worsted. This is probable, however, only in Agathon's sense, when he speaks of the probability of even improbabilities coming to pass. (7) The Chorus too should be regarded as one of the actors; it should be an integral part of the whole, and take a share in the action—that which it has in Sophocles rather than in Euripides. With the later poets, however, the songs in a play of theirs have no more to do with the Plot of that than of any other tragedy. Hence it is that they are now singing intercalary pieces, a practice first introduced by Agathon. And yet what real difference is there between singing such intercalary pieces, and attempting to fit in a speech, or even a whole act, from one play into another?

19

The Plot and Characters having been discussed, it remains to consider the Diction and Thought. As for the Thought, we may assume what is said of it in our Art of Rhetoric, as it belongs more properly to that department of inquiry. The Thought of the personages is shown in everything to be effected by their language—in every effort to prove or disprove, to arouse emotion (pity, fear, anger, and the like), or to maximize or minimize things. It is clear, also, that their mental procedure must be on the same lines in their actions likewise, whenever they wish them to arouse pity or horror, or have a look of importance or probability. The only difference is that with the act the impression has to be made without explanation; whereas with the spoken word it has to be produced by the speaker, and result from his language. What, indeed, would be the good of the speaker, if things appeared in the required light even apart from anything he says?

As regards the Diction, one subject for inquiry under this head is the turns given to the language when spoken; e.g. the difference between command and prayer, simple statement and threat, question and answer, and so forth. The theory of such matters, however, belongs to Elocution and the professors of that art. Whether the poet knows these things or not, his art as a poet is never seriously criticized on that account. What fault can one see in Homer's 'Sing of the wrath, Goddess'?—which Protagoras has criticized as being a command where a prayer was meant, since to bid one do or not do, he tells us, is a command. Let us pass over this, then, as appertaining to another art, and not to that of poetry.

20

The Diction viewed as a whole is made up of the following parts: the Letter (or ultimate element), the Syllable, the Conjunction, the Article, the Noun, the Verb, the Case, and the Speech. (1) The Letter is an indivisible sound of a particular kind, one that may become a factor in an intelligible sound. Indivisible sounds are uttered by the brutes also, but no one of these is a Letter in our sense of the term. These elementary sounds are either vowels, semivowels, or mutes. A vowel is a Letter having an audible sound without the addition of another Letter. A semivowel, one having an audible sound by the addition of another Letter; e.g. S and R. A mute, one having no sound at all by itself, but becoming audible by an addition, that of one of the Letters which have a sound of some sort of their own; e.g. D and G. The Letters differ in various ways: as produced by different conformations or in different regions of the mouth; as aspirated, not aspirated, or sometimes one and sometimes the other; as long, short, or of variable quantity; and further as having an acute grave, or intermediate accent.

The details of these matters we must leave to the metricians. (2) A Syllable is a non-significant composite sound, made up of a mute and a Letter having a sound (a vowel or semivowel); for GR, without an A, is just as much a Syllable as GRA, with an A. The various forms of the Syllable also belong to the theory of metre. (3) A Conjunction is (a) a non-significant sound which, when one significant sound is formable out of several, neither hinders nor aids the union, and which, if the Speech thus formed stands by itself (apart from other Speeches) must not be inserted at the beginning of it; e.g. men, de, toi, de. Or (b) a non-significant sound capable of combining two or more significant sounds into one; e.g. amphi, peri, etc. (4) An Article is a non-significant sound marking the beginning, end, or dividing-point of a Speech, its natural place being either at the extremities or in the middle. (5) A Noun or name is a composite significant sound not involving the idea of time, with parts which have no significance by themselves in it. It is to be remembered that in a compound we do not think of the parts as having a significance also by themselves; in the name 'Theodorus', for instance, the doron means nothing to us.

(6) A Verb is a composite significant sound involving the idea of time, with parts which (just as in the Noun) have no significance by themselves in it. Whereas the word 'man' or 'white' does not imply when, 'walks' and 'has walked' involve in addition to the idea of walking that of time present or time past.

(7) A Case of a Noun or Verb is when the word means 'of or 'to' a thing, and so forth, or for one or many (e.g. 'man' and 'men'); or it may consist merely in the mode of utterance, e.g. in question, command, etc. 'Walked?' and 'Walk!' are Cases of the verb 'to walk' of this last kind. (8) A Speech is a composite significant sound, some of the parts of which have a certain significance by themselves. It may be observed that a Speech is not always made up of Noun and Verb; it may be without a Verb, like the definition of man; but it will always have some part with a certain significance by itself. In the Speech 'Cleon walks', 'Cleon' is an instance of such a part. A Speech is said to be one in two ways, either as signifying one thing, or as a union of several Speeches made into one by conjunction. Thus the Iliad is one Speech by conjunction of several; and the definition of man is one through its signifying one thing.

21

Nouns are of two kinds, either (1) simple, i.e. made up of non-significant parts, like the word γῆ [Greek, (gē) = country], or (2) double; in the latter case the word may be made up either of a significant and a non-significant part (a distinction which disappears in the compound), or of two significant parts. It is possible also to have triple, quadruple or higher compounds, like most of our amplified names; e.g. ' Hermocaicoxanthus' and the like.

Whatever its structure, a Noun must always be either (1) the ordinary word for the thing, or (2) a strange word, or (3) a metaphor, or (4) an ornamental word, or (5) a coined word, or (6) a word lengthened out, or (7) curtailed, or (8) altered in form. By the ordinary word I mean that in general use in a country; and by a strange word, one in use elsewhere. So that the same word may obviously be at once strange and ordinary, though not in reference to the same people; sigunos, for instance, is an ordinary word in Cyprus, and a strange word with us. Metaphor consists in giving the thing a name that belongs to something else; the transference being either from genus to species, or from species to genus, or from species to species, or on grounds of analogy. That from genus to species is eXemplified in 'Here stands my ship'; for lying at anchor is the 'standing' of a particular kind of thing. That from species to genus in 'Truly ten thousand good deeds has Ulysses wrought', where 'ten thousand', which is a particular large number, is put in place of the generic 'a large number'. That from species to species in 'Drawing the life with the bronze', and in 'Severing with the enduring bronze'; where the poet uses 'draw' in the sense of 'sever' and 'sever' in that of 'draw', both words meaning to 'take away' something. That from analogy is possible whenever there are four terms so related that the second (B) is to the first (A), as the fourth (D) to the third (C); for one may then metaphorically put B in lieu of D, and D in lieu of B. Now and then, too, they qualify the metaphor by adding on to it that to which the word it supplants is relative. Thus a cup (B) is in relation to Dionysus (A) what a shield (D) is to Ares (C). The cup accordingly will be metaphorically described as the 'shield of Dionysus' (D + A), and the shield as the 'cup of Ares' (B + C). Or to take another instance: As old age (D) is to life (C), so is evening (B) today (A). One will accordingly describe evening (B) as the 'old age of the day' (D + A)—or by the Empedoclean equivalent; and old age (D) as the 'evening' or 'sunset of life" (B + C). It may be that some of the terms thus related have no special name of their own, but for all that they will be metaphorically described in just the same way. Thus to cast forth seed-corn is called 'sowing'; but to cast forth its flame, as said of the sun, has no special name. This nameless act (B), however, stands in just the same relation to its object, sunlight (A), as sowing (D) to the seed-corn (C). Hence the expression in the poet, 'sowing around a god-created flame' (D + A). There is also another form of qualified metaphor. Having given the thing the alien name, one may by a negative addition deny of it one of the attributes naturally associated with its new name. An instance of this would be to call the shield not the 'cup of Ares,' as in the former case, but a 'cup that holds no wine'. A coined word is a name which, being quite unknown among a people, is given by the poet himself; e.g. (for there are some words that seem to be of this origin) hernyges for horns, and areter for priest. A word is said to be lengthened out, when it has a short vowel made long, or an extra syllable inserted; e. g. polleos for poleos, Peleiadeo for Peleidon. It is said to be curtailed, when it has lost a part; e.g. kri, do, and ops in mia ginetai amphoteron ops. It is an altered word, when part is left as it was and part is of the poet's making; e.g. dexiteron for dexion, in dexiteron kata maxon.

The Nouns themselves (to whatever class they may belong) are either masculine, feminine, or intermediates (neuter). All ending in N, P, S, or in the two compounds of this last, PS and X, are masculine. All ending in the invariably long vowels, H and O, and in A among the vowels that may be long, are feminine. So that there is an equal number of masculine and feminine terminations, as PS and X are the same as S, and need not be counted. There is no Noun, however, ending in a mute or in either of the two short vowels, E and O. Only three (meli, kommi, peperi) end in I, and five in T. The intermediates, or neuters, end in the variable vowels or in N, P, X.

22

The perfection of Diction is for it to be at once clear and not mean. The clearest indeed is that made up of the ordinary words for things, but it is mean, as is shown by the poetry of Cleophon and Sthenelus. On the other hand the Diction becomes distinguished and non-prosaic by the use of unfamiliar terms, i.e. strange words, metaphors, lengthened forms, and everything that deviates from the ordinary modes of speech.—But a whole statement in such terms will be either a riddle or a barbarism, a riddle, if made up of metaphors, a barbarism, if made up of strange words. The very nature indeed of a riddle is this, to describe a fact in an impossible combination of words (which cannot be done with the real names for things, but can be with their metaphorical substitutes); e.g. 'I saw a man glue brass on another with fire', and the like. The corresponding use of strange words results in a barbarism.—A certain admixture, accordingly, of unfamiliar terms is necessary. These, the strange word, the metaphor, the ornamental equivalent, etc. will save the language from seeming mean and prosaic, while the ordinary words in it will secure the requisite clearness. What helps most, however, to render the Diction at once clear and non-prosaic is the use of the lengthened, curtailed, and altered forms of words. Their deviation from the ordinary words will, by making the language unlike that in general use give it a non-prosaic appearance; and their having much in common with the words in general use will give it the quality of clearness. It is not right, then, to condemn these modes of speech, and ridicule the poet for using them, as some have done; e.g. the elder Euclid, who said it was easy to make poetry if one were to be allowed to lengthen the words in the statement itself as much as one likes—a procedure he caricatured by reading 'Epixarhon eidon Marathonade Badi—gonta, and ouk han g' eramenos ton ekeinou helle boron as verses. A too apparent use of these rules has certainly a ludicrous effect, but they are not alone in that; the rule of moderation applies to all the constituents of the poetic vocabulary; even with metaphors, strange words, and the rest, the effect will be the same, if one uses them improperly and with a view to provoking laughter. The proper use of them is a very different thing. To realize the difference one should take an epic verse and see how it reads when the normal words are introduced. The same should be done too with the strange word, the metaphor, and the rest; for one has only to put the ordinary words in their place to see the truth of what we are saying. The same iambic, for instance, is found in Aeschylus and Euripides, and as it stands in the former it is a poor line; whereas Euripides, by the change of a single word, the substitution of a strange for what is by usage the ordinary word, has made it seem a fine one. Aeschylus having said in his Philoctetes:

>phagedaina he mon sarkas hesthiei podos

Euripides has merely altered the hesthiei here into thoinatai. Or suppose

>nun de m' heon holigos te kai outidanos kai haeikos

to be altered by the substitution of the ordinary words into

>nun de m' heon mikros te kai hasthenikos kai haeidos

Or the line

>diphron haeikelion katatheis olingen te trapexan

into

>diphron moxtheron katatheis mikran te trapexan

Or heiones boosin into heiones kraxousin. Add to this that Ariphrades used to ridicule the tragedians for introducing expressions unknown in the language of common life, doeaton hapo (for apo domaton), sethen, hego de nin, Achilleos peri (for peri Achilleos), and the like. The mere fact of their not being in ordinary speech gives the Diction a non-prosaic character; but Ariphrades was unaware of that. It is a great thing, indeed, to make a proper use of these poetical forms, as also of compounds and strange words. But the greatest thing by far is to be a master of metaphor. It is the one thing that cannot be learnt from others; and it is also a sign of genius, since a good metaphor implies an intuitive perception of the similarity in dissimilars.

Of the kinds of words we have enumerated it may be observed that compounds are most in place in the dithyramb, strange words in heroic, and metaphors in iambic poetry. Heroic poetry, indeed, may avail itself of them all. But in iambic verse, which models itself as far as possible on the spoken language, only those kinds of words are in place which are allowable also in an oration, i.e. the ordinary word, the metaphor, and the ornamental equivalent.

Let this, then, suffice as an account of Tragedy, the art imitating by means of action on the stage.

23

As for the poetry which merely narrates, or imitates by means of versified language (without action), it is evident that it has several points in common with Tragedy.

I. The construction of its stories should clearly be like that in a drama; they should be based on a single action, one that is a complete whole in itself, with a beginning, middle, and end, so as to enable the work to produce its own proper pleasure with all the organic unity of a living creature. Nor should one suppose that there is anything like them in our usual histories. A history has to deal not with one action, but with one period and all that happened in that to one or more persons, however disconnected the several events may have been. Just as two events may take place at the same time, e.g. the sea-fight off Salamis and the battle with the Carthaginians in Sicily, without converging to the same end, so too of two consecutive events one may sometimes come after the other with no one end as their common issue. Nevertheless most of our epic poets, one may say, ignore the distinction.

Herein, then, to repeat what we have said before, we have a further proof of Homer's marvelous superiority to the rest. He did not attempt to deal even with the Trojan war in its entirety, though it was a whole with a definite beginning and end—through a feeling apparently that it was too long a story to be taken in in one view, or if not that, too complicated from the variety of incident in it. As it is, he has singled out one section of the whole; many of the other incidents, however, he brings in as episodes, using the Catalogue of the Ships, for instance, and other episodes to relieve the uniformity of his narrative. As for the other epic poets, they treat of one man, or one period; or else of an action which, although one, has a multiplicity of parts in it. This last is what the authors of the Cypria and Little Iliad have done. And the result is that, whereas the Iliad or Odyssey supplies materials for only one, or at most two tragedies, the Cypria does that for several, and the Little Iliad for more than eight: for an Adjudgment of Arms, a Philoctetes, a Neoptolemus, a Eurypylus, a Ulysses as Beggar, a Laconian Women, a Fall of Ilium, and a Departure of the Fleet; as also a Sinon, and Women of Troy.

24

II. Besides this, Epic poetry must divide into the same species as Tragedy; it must be either simple or complex, a story of character or one of suffering. Its parts, too, with the exception of Song and Spectacle, must be the same, as it requires Peripeties, Discoveries, and scenes of suffering just like Tragedy. Lastly, the Thought and Diction in it must be good in their way. All these elements appear in Homer first; and he has made due use of them. His two poems are each examples of construction, the Iliad simple and a story of suffering, the Odyssey complex (there is Discovery throughout it) and a story of character. And they are more than this, since in Diction and Thought too they surpass all other poems.

There is, however, a difference in the Epic as compared with Tragedy, (1) in its length, and (2) in its metre. (1) As to its length, the limit already suggested will suffice: it must be possible for the beginning and end of the work to be taken in in one view—a condition which will be fulfilled if the poem be shorter than the old epics, and about as long as the series of tragedies offered for one hearing. For the extension of its length epic poetry has a special advantage, of which it makes large use. In a play one cannot represent an action with a number of parts going on simultaneously; one is limited to the part on the stage and connected with the actors. Whereas in epic poetry the narrative form makes it possible for one to describe a number of simultaneous incidents; and these, if germane to the subject, increase the body of the poem. This then is a gain to the Epic, tending to give it grandeur, and also variety of interest and room for episodes of diverse kinds. Uniformity of incident by the satiety it soon creates is apt to ruin tragedies on the stage. (2) As for its metre, the heroic has been assigned it from experience; were any one to attempt a narrative poem in some one, or in several, of the other metres, the incongruity of the thing would be apparent. The heroic; in fact is the gravest and weightiest of metres—which is what makes it more tolerant than the rest of strange words and metaphors, that also being a point in which the narrative form of poetry goes beyond all others. The iambic and trochaic, on the other hand, are metres of movement, the one representing that of life and action, the other that of the dance. Still more unnatural would it appear, it one were to write an epic in a medley of metres, as Chaeremon did. Hence it is that no one has ever written a long story in any but heroic verse; nature herself, as we have said, teaches us to select the metre appropriate to such a story.

Homer, admirable as he is in every other respect, is especially so in this, that he alone among epic poets is not unaware of the part to be played by the poet himself in the poem. The poet should say very little in propria persona, as he is no imitator when doing that. Whereas the other poets are perpetually coming forward in person, and say but little, and that only here and there, as imitators, Homer after a brief preface brings in forthwith a man, a woman, or some other Character—no one of them characterless, but each with distinctive characteristics.

The marvelous is certainly required in Tragedy. The Epic, however, affords more opening for the improbable, the chief factor in the marvelous, because in it the agents are not visibly before one. The scene of the pursuit of Hector would be ridiculous on the stage—the Greeks halting instead of pursuing him, and Achilles shaking his head to stop them; but in the poem the absurdity is overlooked. The marvelous, however, is a cause of pleasure, as is shown by the fact that we all tell a story with additions, in the belief that we are doing our hearers a pleasure.

Homer more than any other has taught the rest of us the art of framing lies in the right way. I mean the use of paralogism. Whenever, if A is or happens, a consequent, B, is or happens, men's notion is that, if the B is, the A also is—but that is a false conclusion. Accordingly, if A is untrue, but there is something else, B, that on the assumption of its truth follows as its consequent, the right thing then is to add on the B. Just because we know the truth of the consequent, we are in our own minds led on to the erroneous inference of the truth of the antecedent. Here is an instance, from the Bath-story in the Odyssey.

A likely impossibility is always preferable to an

unconvincing possibility. The story should never be made up of improbable incidents; there should be nothing of the sort in it. If, however, such incidents are unavoidable, they should be outside the piece, like the hero's ignorance in Oedipus of the circumstances of Lams' death; not within it, like the report of the Pythian games in Electra, or the man's having come to Mysia from Tegea without uttering a word on the way, in The Mysians. So that it is ridiculous to say that one's Plot would have been spoilt without them, since it is fundamentally wrong to make up such Plots. If the poet has taken such a Plot, however, and one sees that he might have put it in a more probable form, he is guilty of absurdity as well as a fault of art. Even in the Odyssey the improbabilities in the setting-ashore of Ulysses would be clearly intolerable in the hands of an inferior poet. As it is, the poet conceals them, his other excellences veiling their absurdity. Elaborate Diction, however, is required only in places where there is no action, and no Character or Thought to be revealed. Where there is Character or Thought, on the other hand, an over-ornate Diction tends to obscure them.

25

As regards Problems and their Solutions, one may see the number and nature of the assumptions on which they proceed by viewing the matter in the following way. (1) The poet being an imitator just like the painter or other maker of likenesses, he must necessarily in all instances represent things in one or other of three aspects, either as they were or are, or as they are said or thought to be or to have been, or as they ought to be. (2) All this he does in language, with an admixture, it may be, of strange words and metaphors, as also of the various modified forms of words, since the use of these is conceded in poetry. (3) It is to be remembered, too, that there is not the same kind of correctness in poetry as in politics, or indeed any other art. There is, however, within the limits of poetry itself a possibility of two kinds of error, the one directly, the other only accidentally connected with the art. If the poet meant to describe the thing correctly, and failed through lack of power of expression, his art itself is at fault. But if it was through his having meant to describe it in some incorrect way (e.g. to make the horse in movement have both right legs thrown forward) that the technical error (one in a matter of, say, medicine or some other special science), or impossibilities of whatever kind they may be, have got into his description, his error in that case is not in the essentials of the poetic art. These, therefore, must be the premises of the Solutions in answer to the criticisms involved in the Problems.

I. As to the criticisms relating to the poet's art itself. Any impossibilities there may be in his descriptions of things are faults. But from another point of view they are justifiable, if they serve the end of poetry itself—if (to assume what we have said of that end) they make the effect of some portion of the work more astounding. The Pursuit of Hector is an instance in point. If, however, the poetic end might have been as well or better attained without sacrifice of technical correctness in such matters, the impossibility is not to be justified, since the description should be, if it can, entirely free from error. One may ask, too, whether the error is in a matter directly or only accidentally connected with the poetic art; since it is a lesser error in an artist not to know, for instance, that the hind has no horns, than to produce an unrecognizable picture of one.

II. If the poet's description be criticized as not true to fact, one may urge perhaps that the object ought to be as described—an answer like that of Sophocles, who said that he drew men as they ought to be, and Euripides as they were. If the description, however, be neither true nor of the thing as it ought to be, the answer must be then, that it is in accordance with opinion. The tales about Gods, for instance, may be as wrong as

Xenophanes thinks, neither true nor the better thing to say; but they are certainly in accordance with opinion. Of other statements in poetry one may perhaps say, not that they are better than the truth, but that the fact was so at the time; e.g. the description of the arms: 'their spears stood upright, butt-end upon the ground'; for that was the usual way of fixing them then, as it is still with the Illyrians. As for the question whether something said or done in a poem is morally right or not, in dealing with that one should consider not only the intrinsic quality of the actual word or deed, but also the person who says or does it, the person to whom he says or does it, the time, the means, and the motive of the agent—whether he does it to attain a greater good, or to avoid a greater evil.

III. Other criticisms one must meet by considering the language of the poet: (1) by the assumption of a strange word in a passage like oureas men proton, where by oureas Homer may perhaps mean not mules but sentinels. And in saying of Dolon, hos p e toi eidos men heen kakos, his meaning may perhaps be, not that Dolon's body was deformed, but that his face was ugly, as eneidos is the Cretan word for handsome-faced. So, too, goroteron de keraie may mean not 'mix the wine stronger', as though for topers, but 'mix it quicker'. (2) Other expressions in Homer may be explained as metaphorical; e.g. in halloi men ra theoi te kai aneres eudon (hapantes) pannux as compared with what he tells us at the same time, e toi hot hes pedion to Troikon hathreseien, aulon suriggon *te homadon* the word hapantes 'all', is metaphorically put for 'many', since 'all' is a species of 'many '. So also his oie d' ammoros is metaphorical, the best known standing 'alone'. (3) A change, as Hippias suggested, in the mode of reading a word will solve the difficulty in didomen de oi, and to men ou kataputhetai hombro. (4) Other difficulties may be solved by another punctuation; e.g. in Empedocles, aipsa de thnet ephyonto, ta prin mathon athanata xora te prin kekreto. Or (5) by the assumption of an equivocal term, as in parocheken de pleo nux, where pleo in equivocal. Or (6) by an appeal to the custom of language. Wine-and-water we call 'wine'; and it is on the same principle that Homer speaks of a knemis neoteuktou kassiteroio, a 'greave of new-wrought tin.' A worker in iron we call a 'brazier'; and it is on the same principle that Ganymede is described as the 'wine-server' of Zeus, though the Gods do not drink wine. This latter, however, may be an instance of metaphor. But whenever also a word seems to imply some contradiction, it is necessary to reflect how many ways there may be of understanding it in the passage in question; e.g. in Homer's te r' hesxeto xalkeon hegxos one should consider the possible senses of 'was stopped there'—whether by taking it in this sense or in that one will best avoid the fault of which Glaucon speaks: 'They start with some improbable presumption; and having so decreed it themselves, proceed to draw inferences, and censure the poet as though he had actually said whatever they happen to believe, if his statement conflicts with their own notion of things.' This is how Homer's silence about Icarius has been treated. Starting with, the notion of his having been a Lacedaemonian, the critics think it strange for Telemachus not to have met him when he went to Lacedaemon. Whereas the fact may have been as the Cephallenians say, that the wife of Ulysses was of a Cephallenian family, and that her father's name was Icadius, not Icarius. So that it is probably a mistake of the critics that has given rise to the Problem.

Speaking generally, one has to justify (1) the Impossible by reference to the requirements of poetry, or to the better, or to opinion. For the purposes of poetry a convincing impossibility is preferable to an unconvincing possibility; and if men such as Zeuxis depicted be impossible, the answer is that it is better they should be like that, as the artist ought to improve on his model. (2) The Improbable one has to justify either by showing it to be in accordance with opinion, or by urging that at times it is not improbable; for there is a probability of things happening also against probability. (3) The contradictions found in the poet's language one should first test as one does an opponent's confutation in a dialectical argument, so as to see whether he means the same thing, in the same relation, and in the same sense, before admitting that he has contradicted either something he has said himself or what a man of sound sense assumes as true. But there is no possible apology for improbability of Plot or depravity of character, when they are not necessary and no use is made of them, like the improbability in the appearance of Aegeus in Medea and the baseness of Menelaus in Orestes.

The objections, then, of critics start with faults of five kinds: the allegation is always that something in either (1) impossible, (2) improbable, (3) corrupting, (4) contradictory, or (5) against technical correctness. The answers to these objections must be sought under one or other of the above-mentioned heads, which are twelve in number.

26

The question may be raised whether the epic or the tragic is the higher form of imitation. It may be argued that, if the less vulgar is the higher, and the less vulgar is always that which addresses the better public, an art addressing any and every one is of a very vulgar order. It is a belief that their public cannot see the meaning, unless they add something themselves, that causes the perpetual movements of the performers—bad flute-players, for instance, rolling about, if quoit-throwing is to be represented, and pulling at the conductor, if Scylla is the subject of the piece. Tragedy, then, is said to be an art of this order—to be in fact just what the later actors were in the eyes of their predecessors; for Myrmiscus used to call Callippides 'the ape', because he thought he so overacted his parts; and a similar view was taken of Pindarus also. All Tragedy, however, is said to stand to the Epic as the newer to the older school of actors. The one, accordingly, is said to address a cultivated 'audience, which does not need the accompaniment of gesture; the other, an uncultivated one. If, therefore, Tragedy is a vulgar art, it must clearly be lower than the Epic.

The answer to this is twofold. In the first place, one may urge (1) that the censure does not touch the art of the dramatic poet, but only that of his interpreter; for it is quite possible to overdo the gesturing even in an epic recital, as did Sosistratus, and in a singing contest, as did Mnasitheus of Opus. (2) That one should not condemn all movement, unless one means to condemn even the dance, but only that of ignoble people—which is the point of the criticism passed on Callippides and in the present day on others, that their women are not like gentlewomen. (3) That Tragedy may produce its effect even without movement or action in just the same way as Epic poetry; for from the mere reading of a play its quality may be seen. So that, if it be superior in all other respects, this element of inferiority is not a necessary part of it.

In the second place, one must remember (1) that Tragedy has everything that the Epic has (even the epic metre being admissible), together with a not inconsiderable addition in the shape of the Music (a very real factor in the pleasure of the drama) and the Spectacle. (2) That its reality of presentation is felt in the play as read, as well as in the play as acted. (3) That the tragic imitation requires less space for the attainment of its end; which is a great advantage, since the more concentrated effect is more pleasurable than one with a large admixture of time to dilute it—consider the Oedipus of Sophocles, for instance, and the effect of expanding it into the number of lines of the Iliad. (4) That there is less unity in the imitation of the epic poets, as is proved by the fact that any one work of theirs supplies matter for several tragedies; the result being that, if they take what is really a single story, it seems curt when briefly told, and thin and waterish when on the scale of length usual with their verse. In saying that there is less unity in an epic, I mean an epic made up of a plurality of actions, in the same way as the Iliad and Odyssey have many such parts, each one of them in itself of some magnitude; yet the structure of the two Homeric poems is as perfect as can be, and the action in them is as nearly as possible one action. If, then,

Tragedy is superior in these respects, and also besides these, in its poetic effect (since the two forms of poetry should give us, not any or every pleasure, but the very special kind we have mentioned), it is clear that, as attaining the poetic effect better than the Epic, it will be the higher form of art.

So much for Tragedy and Epic poetry—for these two arts in general and their species; the number and nature of their constituent parts; the causes of success and failure in them; the Objections of the critics, and the Solutions in answer to them.

www.ingramcontent.com/pod-product-compliance
Lightning Source LLC
Chambersburg PA
CBHW021917160426
42813CB00104B/3173/J